THE STORY OF
CIVILIZATION

VOLUME II
THE MEDIEVAL WORLD

TEST BOOK

ISBN: 978-1-5051-0577-3

Published in the United States by
TAN Books
P. O. Box 410487
Charlotte, NC 28241
www.TANBooks.com

Printed in the United States of America.

THE STORY OF
CIVILIZATION

VOLUME II
THE MEDIEVAL WORLD

From the Foundation of Christendom
to the Dawn of the Renaissance

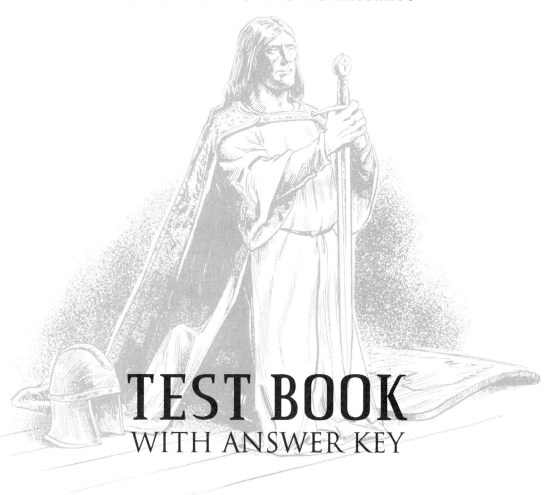

TEST BOOK
WITH ANSWER KEY

CONTENTS

A WORD TO THE TEACHER

This test book serves as a companion resource to *The Story of Civilization: The Medieval World*, authored by Phillip Campbell and brought to you by TAN Books. With this book, students can test their reading comprehension and further educate themselves on the content found in the text.

This volume covers the history of the world from after the days of Constantine's conversion to the earliest days of the Renaissance. Your students will learn what life was like during medieval times as they sack castles and stroll through the muddy roads of small European villages. They'll be introduced to great men of the Church, like Benedict and Patrick who helped spread Christ's kingdom on earth, and step onto the battlefields of history's most famous wars. They'll see the danger the Black Death posed to the world and study medieval literature and architecture. Every step of the way, they will journey to new and exciting places.

The strength of *The Story of Civilization* lies not only in the exciting narrative style in which it retells the historical content but also in the way it presents history through the faithful prism of the Church. Have you always wanted your children to learn about world history from a Catholic perspective? Here, with the textbook and this companion test book, you have the trusted resources you've always wanted.

Enhanced Storytelling

The Story of Civilization reflects a new emphasis in presenting the history of the world as a thrilling and compelling story. Young people love a good story, and history is full of them: from the foundation of Western monasticism by the famous St. Benedict to the capturing of St. Patrick by pirates to the Norman conquest of England to the spread of the Black Death to the adventures of medieval knights.

The storytelling aspect of this series has been especially enhanced in several ways. First, the dynamic style of the new illustrations contributes powerfully to the narrative. Second, an audio recording of the text is available so students can enjoy the stories not just as readers but as listeners as well. This audio recording can assist young students who have not yet acquired the necessary reading vocabulary, as well as students who have reading disabilities. Lastly, the text itself contains short stories within each chapter that help explain the historical content to the children. These stories work in conjunction with the facts, names, dates, and events presented in the text to convey the information in a fun and exciting way.

Using the Test Book

This book provides questions for each chapter that are suitable as a study exercise or as an objective answer test, with an answer key for teachers in the back. The questions include matching items, multiple choice, and true or false, though not every test will contain all these types of questions. Each test is based on a 100-point scale. Students should turn to each test after completing the corresponding textbook chapter and have parents grade it before moving on to the next. Roughly thirty minutes should be given to the student to complete each test, though that may vary depending on the child.

Be sure to visit www.TANBooks.com for more information and other companion products such as activity books, audio dramas, and video lectures.

CHAPTER 1
The Christian Empire

Perfect Score: 100   Your Score: _____

Multiple Choice

Directions: For each numbered item, circle the letter beside the choice (A, B, C, or D) that best answers the question or completes the statement. Circle only one choice per item. Each correct answer is worth 5 points. 25 possible points.

1. Christendom refers to:

A. the times and places where society was based on the Christian religion and the Christian kingdoms were united under the spiritual leadership of the pope.
B. a city where Christ lived.
C. a dome in a basilica.
D. an army of Christian soldiers during the reign of Constantine.

2. The relationship between the Roman Empire and Christian Europe could be compared to:

A. the relationship between a husband and wife.
B. the relationship between a parent and a child.
C. the relationship between Christ and His Church.
D. the relationship between a servant and master.

3. The Edict of Milan:

A. freed the slaves in Rome.
B. put limits on gladiatorial combat.
C. made Christianity legal in the Roman Empire.
D. made Christianity the official religion of the empire.

4. The Hippodrome of Constantinople was:

A. Constantine's imperial senate.
B. a gigantic arena built for chariot racing.
C. a large bridge right outside the city.
D. the biggest hippo museum in the world.

5. Before Constantine, many Christian churches:

A. were made of simple bricks.
B. were blue and white.
C. had no windows.
D. were inside peoples' homes.

True or False?

Directions: In the blank beside each statement, write "T" if the statement is *True* or "F" if the statement is *False*. Each correct answer is worth 5 points. 25 possible points.

_____ 1. At first, Christian Europe retained the laws, culture, and organization of the Roman Empire.

_____ 2. Wherever Christianity spread, it was understood and accepted without error.

_____ 3. Arianism was a heresy that taught Jesus Christ did not suffer and die for us.

_____ 4. Constantine, the emperor in the west, defeated Licinius, the emperor of the east.

_____ 5. Julian was the last pagan emperor.

Matching

Directions: In each blank beside a phrase, write the letter of the term that is described by that phrase. Each item is worth 5 points. 50 possible points.

A. basilica
B. Byzantium
C. Arianism
D. ecumenical council

E. the Nicene Creed
F. Julian the apostate
G. apostate
H. Constantine

I. Saint Ambrose
J. Theodosius

_____ 1. when bishops from the entire universal Church, in union with and in submission to the pope, gather in a meeting to discuss matters of doctrine and discipline

_____ 2. the first Christian emperor

_____ 3. a very large or important church

_____ 4. a heresy condemned at the Council of Nicaea

_____ 5. written at the Council of Nicaea

_____ 6. Christianity became the official religion of the Roman Empire during his reign.

_____ 7. a Christian who abandons Christianity

_____ 8. renamed Constantinople and made the capital of the empire

_____ 9. insisted that the emperor Theodosius repent after he unjustly slaughtered over seven thousand men

_____ 10. pagan emperor and nephew of Constantine

CHAPTER 2
The End of the Roman World

Perfect Score: 100   Your Score: _____

Matching

Directions: In each blank beside a phrase, write the letter of the term that is described by that phrase. Each item is worth 5 points. 50 possible points.

A. Alaric
B. Romulus Augustulus
C. Saint Augustine
D. Doctor of the Church
E. Huns

F. Justa Grata Honoria
G. Aëtius
H. Pope Leo I
I. Visigoths
J. Attila

_____ 1. the sister of the Emperor Valentinian III, who sent a letter to Attila with a ring asking him to save her from an undesirable arranged marriage

_____ 2. Attila's meeting with him convinced Attila to retreat from Italy.

_____ 3. the leader of the Visigoths

_____ 4. the last Roman emperor of the west

_____ 5. one of the most feared barbarian tribes

_____ 6. After his death, the Huns were no longer a real threat.

_____ 7. a person whose spiritual writings are so insightful that they are recommended to all Christians as a sure guide for their faith

_____ 8. Roman general who forced Attila to retreat from Gaul

_____ 9. sacked Rome

_____ 10. wrote *The City of God*

True or False?

Directions: In the blank beside each statement, write "T" if the statement is *True* or "F" if the statement is *False*. Each correct answer is worth 5 points. 50 possible points.

_____ 1. The emperors were still ruling from Rome at the time the Vandals sacked the city.

_____ 2. Saint Augustine wrote, "If one is good in this world, it is guaranteed that one will always receive material blessings."

_____ 3. Attila invaded Gaul, threatening to take Honoria away as his wife and seize all of the western empire for his own.

_____ 4. After the barbarians sacked Ravenna in 476, the Roman Empire would continue in the East for some centuries longer, but it faded in the West.

_____ 5. Emperor Valentinian was very kind and forgiving to his sister.

_____ 6. Alaric spared the Christian basilicas because he was afraid of the Christian God.

_____ 7. The Romans were shaken by the sack of Rome in 410.

_____ 8. In Augustine's life, barbarians began overrunning parts of the Roman Empire.

_____ 9. After the death of Theodosius, the empire was again split into western and eastern halves, each with its own emperor.

_____ 10. The last Roman emperor in the west was deposed by Odoacer.

CHAPTER 3
The Age of Justinian

Perfect Score: 100   Your Score: _____

Multiple Choice

Directions: For each numbered item, circle the letter beside the choice (A, B, C, or D) that best answers the question or completes the statement. Circle only one choice per item. Each correct answer is worth 5 points. 75 possible points.

1. The capital of the eastern Roman Empire was:

A. Athens.
B. Constantinople.
C. Hippodrome.
D. Ravenna.

2. Justinian's ambition as emperor was to:

A. reconquer the west from the barbarian tribes.
B. end gladiatorial combat.
C. discourage revolts.
D. build beautiful churches.

3. Justinian had a very able general named:

A. Alaric.
B. Theodore.
C. Belisarius.
D. Attila.

4. After the Ostrogothic Kingdom was finally destroyed, much of the Italian countryside was:

A. wrecked by the war.
B. still overrun with barbarians.
C. pagan.
D. plagued with disease.

5. This document took all the imperial laws that had been issued over the past four hundred years and put them into a single book.

A. Magna Carta
B. the code of Hammurabi
C. Roman Law
D. the Justinian Code

6. The famous Nika Revolt of 532:

A. broke out during a chariot race in the Hippodrome.
B. was unorganized but successfully overthrew Justinian.
C. destroyed the Hippodrome.
D. was stopped by Pope Leo.

7. Justinian's most lasting contribution was:

A. to Roman architecture.
B. his law code.
C. his defeat of the barbarians in the West.
D. his restrictions on gladiatorial combat.

8. Justinian tried to conquer the barbarians by:

A. sending Pope Leo to negotiate.
B. praying to God.
C. using military force.
D. bringing elephants into combat.

9. The word *nika* means:

A. energy.
B. victory.
C. defeat.
D. unity.

10. Justinian's wife was:

A. Theodora.
B. Cleopatra.
C. Roxanna.
D. Helena.

11. The two most famous chariot racing teams in Constantinople were:

A. the Blacks and the Whites.
B. the Cubs and the White stockings.
C. the Reds and the Whites.
D. the Blues and the Greens.

12. The most popular sport during the reign of Justinian was:

A. swimming.
B. chariot racing.
C. fencing.
D. archery.

13. The last Latin speaking emperor of Constantinople was:

A. Belisarius.
B. Constantine.
C. Justinian I.
D. Julian.

14. By Justinian's time, there were no more:

A. chariot races.
B. gladiatorial fights.
C. basilicas.
D. riots.

15. Justinian's wars against the barbarians were:

A. successful at first, though later the West was lost again.
B. totally unsuccessful.
C. disorganized and poorly planned.
D. successful in permanently winning back the West.

True or False?

Directions: In the blank beside each statement, write "T" if the statement is *True* or "F" if the statement is *False*. Each correct answer is worth 5 points. 25 possible points.

_____ 1. Several riots broke out during the reign of Justinian.

_____ 2. Justinian was completely successful in everything he did.

_____ 3. Many people were unhappy with Justinian. They believed his taxes were too high and they disliked the law code.

_____ 4. After the West was taken over by barbarians, the eastern Roman Empire endured.

_____ 5. Justinian and his wife always agreed on things.

CHAPTER 4
The Rule of St. Benedict

Perfect Score: 100					Your Score: _____

Matching

Directions: In each blank beside a phrase, write the letter of the term that is described by that phrase. Each item is worth 5 points. 50 possible points.

A. monk
B. monasteries
C. Rule of St. Benedict
D. udleness
E. abbot

F. Scholastica
G. nuns
H. Monte Cassino
I. cowl
J. Benedictines

_____ 1. women who live the monastic life

_____ 2. meant to govern how life went on in the monastery: who should do what jobs, what prayers should be prayed, and how the monks should conduct themselves

_____ 3. a rough monastic hood

_____ 4. those who follow Benedict's rule

_____ 5. a man who dedicates his life to serving God by practicing poverty, chastity, and obedience

_____ 6. Benedict's sister who started a monastic way of life for women

_____ 7. the superior of a monastery

_____ 8. Benedict's largest monastery was at this place.

_____ 9. special buildings made just for monastic living

_____ 10. Benedict thought this was bad for the soul.

True or False?

Directions: In the blank beside each statement, write "T" if the statue is *True* or "F" if the statement is *False*. Each correct answer is worth 5 points. 50 possible points.

_____ 1. The manual and spiritual labor of the monks contributed very little to civilization.

_____ 2. Benedict performed many miracles, one of which involved a monk walking on water by Benedict's intercession to save another monk from drowning.

_____ 3. The monasteries became places of learning that preserved much of the writing of the ancient world.

_____ 4. St. Benedict saw that the riches of this world were of great value.

_____ 5. While Roman culture in the west was collapsing, St. Benedict was setting out to rebuild civilization in his own way.

_____ 6. After his studies, Benedict left home to seek a sinful life of worldly pleasure.

_____ 7. Benedict was inspired by the stories of men like St. Anthony of Egypt and St. Paul the Hermit.

_____ 8. Benedict believed that monks should always live alone.

_____ 9. Benedict's rule was not very popular. It made it harder for regular people to serve God in the monastic life.

_____ 10. The work and study of the monks was broken up by community prayers eight times throughout the day and night.

CHAPTER 5
The Irish Missions

Perfect Score: 100   Your Score: _____

Matching

Directions: In each blank beside a phrase, write the letter of the term that is described by that phrase. Each item is worth 5 points. 50 possible points.

A. Ireland

B. Gaelic

C. Druids

D. missionary

E. Irish Gaels

F. St. Patrick

G. St. Brigid

H. St. Enda

I. St. Columba

J. Irish monks

_____ 1. a small island to the west of Britain

_____ 2. a companion of St. Patrick who founded the first convent for nuns in Ireland under the great oak tree at Kildare

_____ 3. the language spoken by the Irish Gaels

_____ 4. a Christian who goes to a pagan land to spread the teachings of Jesus Christ

_____ 5. They worked hard making copies of the Scriptures, writings of the Church Fathers, and other ancient works.

_____ 6. the Apostle of Ireland

_____ 7. the most powerful group in pagan Ireland; they practiced magic and knew the lore of the ancient gods and spirits of the Gaels

_____ 8. A generation after St. Patrick, this Irish warrior gave up violence and retreated to an island called Aran Mor where he founded a famous monastery school.

_____ 9. the Apostle of Scotland

_____ 10. lived in small villages scattered throughout the island ruled by several different kings

True or False?

Directions: In the blank beside each statement, write "T" if the statement is *True* or "F" if the statement is *False*. Each correct answer is worth 5 points. 50 possible points.

____ 1. Ireland was never part of the Roman Empire.

____ 2. Patrick's family was Christian; his father was a deacon, and other members of his family belonged to the clergy.

____ 3. Irish raiders kidnapped Patrick and took him back to Ireland as a slave.

____ 4. Upon returning to Ireland, Patrick was confronted by the Druids, who were very welcoming and friendly to the gospel.

____ 5. After six years in captivity, God sent Patrick a dream and told him a ship was waiting to take him to freedom.

____ 6. Patrick turned away from God in his captivity.

____ 7. Like St. Benedict, Patrick was a wonder-worker.

____ 8. After returning home, Patrick had a dream where God told him to return to Ireland as a missionary.

____ 9. The Irish monks observed the Benedictine rule.

____ 10. Patrick went to Rome to study and was ordained a priest and then bishop.

CHAPTER 6
The Church's Eldest Daughter

Perfect Score: 100   Your Score: _____

Matching

Directions: In each blank beside a phrase, write the letter of the term that is described by that phrase. Each item is worth 5 points. 50 possible points.

A. St. Clotilde   F. King Clovis
B. Franks   G. France
C. Merovingians   H. the Church's eldest daughter
D. Arianism   I. the Burgundians
E. Clodomir   J. Remigius

_____ 1. The Frankish Kingdom Clovis had built was later known as this.

_____ 2. The Frankish kings of Clovis' family were called this.

_____ 3. had once been a pagan tribe, but some had converted to Christianity

_____ 4. the second child of Clovis and Clotilde

_____ 5. the daughter of the king of Burgundy and wife of Clovis

_____ 6. He was the first Christian king of the Franks.

_____ 7. Most of the Franks were pagans, but some had converted to this heresy.

_____ 8. France is sometimes called this because it was the first of the barbarian kingdoms to convert to the Faith.

_____ 9. Clovis was quite fond of this bishop.

_____ 10. After the fall of the western Roman Empire, Gaul was invaded by these pagan barbarians.

Multiple Choice

Directions: For each numbered item, circle the letter beside the choice (A, B, C, or D) that best answers the question or completes the statement. Circle only one choice per item. Each correct answer is worth 5 points. 25 possible points.

1. Clovis blamed and resented the Christian God for:

A. the death of his firstborn child.
B. a disease that spread in his kingdom.
C. famine.
D. terrible floods that happened on feast days.

2. After the reign of Clovis, paganism and the Arian heresy:

A. spread significantly to other lands.
B. remained just as popular.
C. grew more popular in Gaul.
D. began to die out in Gaul.

3. Clovis converted after:

A. God appeared to him in a dream.
B. his prayers to Jesus Christ were answered in battle, and he was granted victory.
C. Clotilde and the bishop of Reims convinced him with logical arguments of the truth of Christianity.
D. he was miraculously healed from a deadly disease.

4. After Clovis' death, the Merovingian family:

A. continued to be faithful to the Church.
B. persecuted Christians.
C. went back to its pagan ways.
D. destroyed the Christian churches.

5. After her father decided to marry her to a pagan man, Clotilde:

A. tried to run away from home.
B. prayed and fasted a great deal in the hope that God might cause her father to change his mind.
C. accepted her father's decision as God's will and went freely.
D. lost her faith in God.

True or False?

Directions: In the blank beside each statement, write "T" if the statement is *True* or "F" if the statement is *False*. Each correct answer is worth 5 points. 25 possible points.

_____ 1. After they were married, Clovis and Clotilde grew to love each other.

_____ 2. Clovis was a pagan, so he did not allow Clotilde to practice her faith.

_____ 3. In battle, Clovis prayed to the pagan gods of the Franks, and they always granted him victory.

_____ 4. The Merovingian kings were fierce warriors who kept their beards and hair long and flowing as a symbol of their kingship.

_____ 5. Clovis and Clotilde's first child was born and baptized, but immediately after being baptized, he got sick and died.

CHAPTER 7
The Coming of the Moors

Perfect Score: 100   Your Score: _____

True or False?

Directions: In the blank beside each statement, write "T" if the statement is *True* or "F" if the statement is *False*. Each correct answer is worth 5 points. 25 possible points.

_____ 1. Leander and St. Isidore were brothers who helped bring about the conversion of Visigothic kings.

_____ 2. Muhammad converted his family to the new faith, but the pagan Arabs disliked Muhammad's teaching and drove him into exile.

_____ 3. There are no pieces of truth in any other religions besides Catholicism.

_____ 4. The Muslims rejected that Jesus was the Son of God. They said he was simply a prophet, but inferior to Muhammad.

_____ 5. It took centuries for the followers of Muhammad to seize power, and they did so peacefully.

Matching

Directions: In each blank beside a phrase, write the letter of the term that is described by that phrase. Each item is worth 5 points. 75 possible points.

A. St. Isidore
B. caravans
C. Visigothic kings
D. Arabs
E. Muhammad
F. Islam
G. Muslims
H. Caliph
I. Moors
J. Quran
K. Roderic
L. Sisibert
M. Pelayo
N. Asturias
O. the Trinity

_____ 1. a largely nomadic people who lived in the dry, hot lands of the Arabian Peninsula on the outskirts of the Byzantine Empire

_____ 2. often spent their time fighting amongst each other or against their nobles, thus dividing the kingdom

_____ 3. became one of Spain's most popular saints

_____ 4. the only Christian kingdom left in Spain after the Muslims took over

_____ 5. a word that means "submission"

_____ 6. the political and religious head of the Islamic religion

_____ 7. those who follow Islam

_____ 8. Muslims who invaded and settled Spain were called _____.

_____ 9. large groups of merchants who loaded their goods on wagons or camels

_____ 10. The caliphs who followed Muhammad compiled all his sayings into this book, which became the holy book of Islam.

_____ 11. the Visigothic king at the time that the Muslims attacked

_____ 12. a pagan merchant from a city called Mecca, who claimed that an angel told him that there was only one God called Allah in Arabic

_____ 13. a high ranking noble who betrayed King Roderic

_____ 14. a Christian doctrine that Muslims reject

_____ 15. a Visigothic noble who refused to pay the tax to his Muslim overlords and retreated to the mountains with a band of warriors

CHAPTER 8
The Carolingians

Perfect Score: 100   Your Score: _____

True or False?

Directions: In the blank beside each statement, write "T" if the statement is *True* or "F" if the statement is *False*. Each correct answer is worth 5 points. 50 possible points.

_____ 1. The descendants of Clovis were not as powerful as he had been.

_____ 2. When he heard of the Moorish threat, Charles Martel became afraid and did nothing to counter the attack.

_____ 3. Charles Martel's son, Pepin the Short, like his father, began as mayor of the palace.

_____ 4. Pepin got sick of having to be second-in-command to a useless king.

_____ 5. Pope Zachary issued a papal bull confirming that it was proper for a king to reign even if he had no power.

_____ 6. The Carolingian Empire was divided in the time of Charlemagne's grandsons.

_____ 7. Pepin gave much land in central Italy to the papacy to be the Church's own territory.

_____ 8. Charlemagne was not religious and therefore not a friend of the Church.

_____ 9. Charlemagne's long reign was mostly uneventful, and he conquered very little.

_____ 10. On Christmas day of the year 800, while Charlemagne was praying at Mass, Pope Leo crowned him Roman emperor.

Multiple Choice

Directions: For each numbered item, circle the letter beside the choice (A, B, C, or D) that best answers the question or completes the statement. Circle only one choice per item. Each correct answer is worth 5 points. 50 possible points.

1. A papal bull is:

A. a cow owned by the pope.
B. a document issued by the pope about some important matter.
C. a letter from the pope to a bishop.
D. an infallible doctrine of the Faith.

2. Pepin used the words of the pope to support him in his plan to:

A. murder his father.
B. assassinate the king.
C. excommunicate the king.
D. have the Merovingian king deposed and sent to a monastery.

3. After his crowning by Pope Leo, Charlemagne went by the title:

A. king.
B. bishop.
C. emperor.
D. "Charles the Great."

4. When Pepin died:

A. the kingdom of the Franks fell into ruin.
B. his son Charles succeeded him as king of the Franks.
C. the Vikings took over.
D. his sons fought over his throne for more than five years.

5. The Franks called Charles "Charlemagne", which means:

A. "Charles the Great."
B. "king of the Franks."
C. "conqueror of barbarians."
D. "Charles the pious."

6. The lands in Italy that Pepin gave to the Church were known as:

A. the Papal States.
B. the Roman Provinces.
C. the Italian City-states.
D. the Holy Territories.

7. The word *Renaissance* means:

A. "beginning."
B. "holy art."
C. "holiness."
D. "rebirth."

8. The family of Charles Martel, Pepin, and Charlemagne is called:

A. the Carolingians.
B. the Charlemagne dynasty.
C. the holy kings.
D. the Merovingians.

9. The period of great learning and building associated with the reign of Charlemagne and his sons is called:

A. the Roman Renewal.
B. the Educational Reform.
C. the Carolingian Renaissance.
D. the Latin Resurrection.

10. Charles Martel's bearded, battle-ax-carrying Franks fought the Muslim Moors and dealt them a crushing defeat at the battle of:

A. Rome.
B. Tours.
C. Constantinople.
D. Florence.

CHAPTER 9
The Conversion of Europe

Perfect Score: 100   Your Score: _____

Matching

Directions: In each blank beside a phrase, write the letter of the term that is described by that phrase. Each item is worth 5 points. 50 possible points.

A. missionary   F. Anskar
B. St. Boniface   G. Balkans
C. Bible   H. Slavs
D. Scandinavia   I. St. Cyril
E. Vikings   J. apostles to the Slavs

_____ 1. a land north of Germany

_____ 2. These people settled in the Balkans around the time the Roman Empire was collapsing.

_____ 3. St. Boniface was eventually martyred while holding _____.

_____ 4. someone who is sent forth to bring others to the Christian faith

_____ 5. Scandinavia was home to various tribes of pagan warriors called _____.

_____ 6. St. Cyril and St. Methodius are remembered as _____.

_____ 7. To the east and south of Germany is a mountainous region known as _____.

_____ 8. a Frankish missionary monk who spent years among the people of Scandinavia preaching the gospel and building churches

_____ 9. He studied the Slavic language and invented an alphabet and a writing system for the Slavs.

_____ 10. famously chopped down the sacred oak tree of Thor

True or False?

Directions: In the blank beside each statement, write "T" if the statement is *True* or "F" if the statement is *False*. Each correct answer is worth 5 points. 50 possible points.

_____ 1. The Christian monks were not able to earn the barbarians' trust.

_____ 2. St. Boniface taught the barbarians in Germany the gospel of Jesus Christ, built churches, and became their bishop.

_____ 3. The Bible that St. Boniface was holding when he died has been preserved.

_____ 4. St. Anskar is known as the Apostle to the North.

_____ 5. St. Anskar is sometimes depicted holding a church building to signify his success at founding churches.

_____ 6. The Slavs had a written language; therefore, it was easy for them to learn about God through written texts.

_____ 7. After the fall of the Roman Empire, there were many pagan barbarians who invaded and settled throughout Europe.

_____ 8. Saints Cyril and Methodius had the Scriptures and other Christian writings translated into the Slavic alphabet so the common people could learn the Faith.

_____ 9. In the early Middle Ages, most missionaries were just ordinary laymen.

_____ 10. St. Boniface was sent by the pope to preach to various pagan tribes living in central and northern Germany.

CHAPTER 10
Anglo-Saxon England

Perfect Score: 100   Your Score: _____

Matching

Directions: In each blank beside a phrase, write the letter of the term that is described by that phrase. Each item is worth 5 points. 50 possible points.

A. Britain   F. England
B. Vortigern   G. St. Augustine of Canterbury
C. mercenaries   H. Danish Vikings
D. King Alfred   I. Anglo-Saxons
E. Heptarchy   J. pagans

_____ 1. the collective name given to the seven kingdoms of Britain

_____ 2. The old British were Christians, but the Anglo-Saxons were _____.

_____ 3. the leader of Britain at the time the Anglo-Saxons invaded

_____ 4. He famously encountered a country woman who did not know he was the king.

_____ 5. soldiers who work for hire

_____ 6. Kind Alfred of Wessex spent most of his reign battling them.

_____ 7. Pope Gregory the Great sent this Benedictine monk to evangelize England.

_____ 8. an island off the northwest coast of Europe

_____ 9. Two of Vortigern's mercenaries were Hengist and Horsa, who belonged to this pagan barbarian tribe.

_____ 10. After the Anglo-Saxons took over, this nation was renamed.

Multiple Choice

Directions: For each numbered item, circle the letter beside the choice (A, B, C, or D) that best answers the question or completes the statement. Circle only one choice per item. Each correct answer is worth 5 points. 25 possible points.

1. Vortigern did his best, but without the Romans, he did not have:

A. a large enough army to fight the pagans.
B. enough supplies to aid his efforts.
C. large enough boats.
D. the strength it took to maintain power.

2. Hengist and Horsa were invited to bring their tribe over to settle in Britain on the condition that:

A. they would help gather food.
B. they would not live as equal citizens with the Britains.
C. they would fight for Vortigern.
D. they would convert to Christianity.

3. It soon became clear to Vortigern that Hengist and Horsa planned to:

A. steal supplies from the Britains.
B. use their tribe to take over his kingdom.
C. eavesdrop on the king.
D. convert to Christianity.

4. This famous monk was an example of a converted Anglo-Saxon who became a great missionary.

A. St. Boniface
B. St. Anskar
C. St. Augustine of Hippo
D. St. Augustine of Canterbury

5. Beginning in the late eighth century, these pagans began to attack the east coast of England.

A. Anglo-Saxons
B. Germanic tribes
C. Byzantines
D. Danish Vikings

True or False?

Directions: In the blank beside each statement, write "T" if the statement is *True* or "F" if the statement is *False*. Each correct answer is worth 5 points. 25 possible points.

_____ 1. The British and the Anglo-Saxons had several battles, but the British were victorious in the end.

_____ 2. The Anglo-Saxon kings who succeeded Alfred were not as popular, powerful, or pious.

_____ 3. After converting, the Viking king Guthrum still made war on Alfred.

_____ 4. After the fall of the Roman Empire, pagan tribes from Scotland were attacking Britain from the north and Irish raiders from the west.

_____ 5. Hengist and Horsa became kings and divided Britain up among the Anglo-Saxons.

CHAPTER 11
The Normans

Perfect Score: 100   Your Score: _____

Matching

Directions: In each blank beside a phrase, write the letter of the term that is described by that phrase. Each item is worth 5 points. 50 possible points.

A. monasteries   F. Normans
B. Rollo   G. chain mail
C. Charles the Simple   H. lance
D. Normandy   I. right of sanctuary
E. Mont Saint-Michel   J. St. Aubert

_____ 1. a very long spear meant to be used from horseback

_____ 2. Norse leader who led the attack against France

_____ 3. The land in which the Norse spread throughout northern France became known as _____.

_____ 4. was visited by St. Michael and asked to build an abbey in a specific location

_____ 5. a Benedictine abbey that rises five hundred feet above the sea level atop a rocky island off the coast of Normandy

_____ 6. the most powerful and feared warriors of the high Middle Ages

_____ 7. an armor suit made up of thousands of tiny interlocking metal rings

_____ 8. At the time of the Norse invasions, France was ruled by this descendant of Charlemagne.

_____ 9. meant that anybody could hide inside a church building and nobody could use violence to bring them out

_____ 10. These were special targets for Vikings to plunder because of the gold liturgical vessels and precious books they contained.

True or False?

Directions: In the blank beside each statement, write "T" if the statement is *True* or "F" if the statement is *False*. Each correct answer is worth 5 points. 50 possible points.

_____ 1. The skull of St. Aubert is still preserved today.

_____ 2. The Normans were very peaceful and not prone to fighting.

_____ 3. The Vikings consisted of three main groups: the Danes, the Swedes, and the Norse.

_____ 4. For a long time, there was war between Charles and Rollo before they made peace.

_____ 5. The Normans embraced Christianity reluctantly and with little enthusiasm.

_____ 6. The Norman warriors were best known for their heavy lances.

_____ 7. The Normans stayed among themselves and did not settle abroad.

_____ 8. The Normans loved battle.

_____ 9. The Church said that nobody should fight on Sundays and holy days.

_____ 10. St. Michael appeared to St. Aubert and put a hole in his head with his finger to remind Aubert to build the abbey of Mont Saint-Michel.

CHAPTER 12
The Norman Conquest of England

Perfect Score: 100   Your Score: _____

Matching

Directions: In each blank beside a phrase, write the letter of the term that is described by that phrase. Each item is worth 5 points. 50 possible points.

A. King Ethelred the Unready
B. St. Edward
C. tapestry
D. Harold Godwinson
E. shield wall

F. Duke William of Normandy
G. Tower of London
H. Normandy
I. Danes
J. Hastings

_____ 1. The Anglo-Saxons were famous for this battle formation.

_____ 2. Ethelred's son, who was a just and pious ruler

_____ 3. This descendant of Alfred was driven from his throne by the Danes, after which he fled to Normandy to stay with his wife's family while the Danes ruled England.

_____ 4. St. Edward was raised here.

_____ 5. an embroidered cloth, often with pictures or designs that told a story

_____ 6. the Norman leader who invaded and conquered England, becoming its king in 1066

_____ 7. The Norman and Anglo-Saxon armies battled here in October 1066.

_____ 8. a massive fortress built by King William that still exists today

_____ 9. The Anglo-Saxon nobles wanted this man to be their king.

_____ 10. Immediately after being crowned, Harold had a great victory over this group.

Multiple Choice

Directions: For each numbered item, circle the letter beside the choice (A, B, C, or D) that best answers the question or completes the statement. Circle only one choice per item. Each correct answer is worth 5 points. 25 possible points.

1. When William rescued Harold from a shipwreck in Normandy, William told him that:

A. King Edward had promised to leave the throne to him when he died.
B. he was his father.
C. he was secretly plotting to take over England.
D. King Edward had an illegitimate child who was heir to the throne.

2. When he returned to take the throne of England, Edward:

A. was greeted joyfully.
B. became severely Anglo-Saxon, despite his Norman heritage.
C. brought his Norman friends with him.
D. created many important new laws.

3. King Harold Goodwinson died from:

A. poisoning.
B. an arrow through his eye.
C. drowning.
D. a sharp blow from an ax.

4. William became known as:

A. William the Pious.
B. William the Great.
C. William the Conqueror.
D. William the Just.

5. William commemorated his victory over Harold by:

A. staging a massive military parade through London.
B. setting off fireworks.
C. having a large tapestry woven depicting his victory.
D. having poems written about his victory.

True or False?

Directions: In the blank beside each statement, write "T" if the statement is *True* or "F" if the statement is *False*. Each correct answer is worth 5 points. 25 possible points.

_____ 1. The Anglo-Saxon nobles were very pleased with St. Edward.

_____ 2. William refused to allow Harold to return to England until Harold promised to support William's claim to the English throne.

_____ 3. St. Edward summoned Harold Godwinson to his deathbed and made him his heir.

_____ 4. It is very clear to all historians that St. Edward made both William and Harold his heirs.

_____ 5. William tricked the Anglo-Saxons into breaking their shield wall and then attacked them when they were vulnerable.

CHAPTER 13
The Crusades

Perfect Score: 100   Your Score: _____

Matching

Directions: In each blank beside a phrase, write the letter of the term that is described by that phrase. Each item is worth 5 points. 75 possible points.

A. Saladin
B. military order
C. excommunicated
D. crusader
E. schism
F. Michael Cerularius
G. Seljuk Turks
H. Alexius Comnenus

I. Antioch
J. Godfrey de Bouillon
K. The Third Crusade
L. The Second Crusade
M. Kingdom of Jerusalem
N. Pope Urban II
O. Horns of Hattin

_____ 1. A person who went to fight the Muslims in the Holy Land was called this, which means "cross bearer."

_____ 2. the bishop of Constantinople who was excommunicated by the papal legates sent by Leo IX

_____ 3. This is often known as the "King's Crusade."

_____ 4. This crusading conqueror of Jerusalem took the title "Defender of the Holy Sepulcher."

_____ 5. Emperor Alexius broke his oath and refused to give the crusaders supplies when they attacked this Syrian city.

_____ 6. a band of knights who took religious vows, known as "fighting monks"

_____ 7. a determined opponent of the crusaders who wanted to end the Kingdom of Jerusalem and restore it to Muslim rule

_____ 8. This Byzantine emperor was afraid of the Seljuk Turks and reached out to the West, asking the pope to recruit some knights to help free the Christians suffering under Seljuk oppression.

_____ 9. when people refuse obedience to the pope and will not hold communion with the Church

_____ 10. In the 1000s, this new barbarian tribe came out of Asia and began attacking Byzantine lands in the East and harassing the Christian pilgrims who visited the Holy Land.

_____ 11. The crusaders were annihilated by Saladin in this battle.

_____ 12. This was launched in 1145 after Edessa, one of the crusader states, fell to the Muslims.

_____ 13. to be removed from communion with the Church and deprived of the sacraments

_____ 14. The First Crusade was summoned by _____.

_____ 15. the crusader state in the Holy Land, composed of four separate kingdoms

Multiple Choice

Directions: For each numbered item, circle the letter beside the choice (A, B, C, or D) that best answers the question or completes the statement. Circle only one choice per item. Each correct answer is worth 5 points. 25 possible points.

1. After the crusades, the Templar Knights became some of the most important _____ of the high Middle Ages.

A. bankers
B. farmers
C. swordsmen
D. blacksmiths

2. Pope Urban II thought helping Emperor Alexius would be a good way to:

A. gain secular power.
B. renew religious zeal.
C. create an acceptable pretense for waging war against the Muslims.
D. repair relations with Constantinople and the Greek Church.

3. Alexius made the crusaders promise that they would turn over any reconquered lands to him. In exchange for this, Alexius promised to:

A. give the crusaders supplies when they needed them.
B. send Byzantine warriors to add to their forces.
C. let them keep half of their spoils.
D. protect their families while they were away.

4. These were formed to protect travelers going to the Holy Land from Muslim attacks.

A. secret entrances to the Holy Land
B. alliances with the Seljuk Turks
C. military orders
D. walls around the city of Jerusalem

5. The Greek Christians of Sicily were offended by the Normans because:

A. they were too friendly with the Muslims.
B. the Normans tried to make them adopt Norman customs of worship.
C. they grew their hair long like barbarians.
D. they drank lots of alcohol.

CHAPTER 14
The Investiture Controversy

Perfect Score: 100   Your Score: _____

Matching

Directions: In each blank beside a phrase, write the letter of the term that is described by that phrase. Each item is worth 5 points. 50 possible points.

A. Gelasius
B. concordat
C. Otto the Great
D. the Holy Roman Empire
E. simony

F. lay investiture
G. Hildebrand
H. Henry IV
I. Concordat of Worms
J. Canossa

_____ 1. Around the time of the fall of the Roman Empire, this pope wrote about the relationship between the Church and state.

_____ 2. a tenth-century king who reigned from 936 to 973 and made Germany a very powerful kingdom

_____ 3. Emperor Henry IV spent three days doing penance here before Pope Gregory agreed to speak with him.

_____ 4. After the Pope crowned him, Otto's German empire was known as _____.

_____ 5. an agreement the Church enters into with the government of a nation

_____ 6. the practice of a new bishop receiving his staff and ring from his temporal lord, who was a layman

_____ 7. the buying and selling of Church offices or spiritual goods

_____ 8. This Holy Roman emperor is famous for his conflict with Pope Gregory VII over lay investiture.

_____ 9. This agreement between Pope Callixtus II and Emperor Henry V said bishops could not receive their staff and ring from their lord because these were signs of their spiritual office.

_____ 10. This reforming monk was elected pope and took the name Gregory VII.

Multiple Choice

Directions: For each numbered item, circle the letter beside the choice (A, B, C, or D) that best answers the question or completes the statement. Circle only one choice per item. Each correct answer is worth 5 points. 25 possible points.

1. Henry IV's nobles did not want to serve an emperor who:

A. was so poorly trained for battle.
B. had such poor manners.
C. was not for certain the rightful successor.
D. was kicked out of the Church.

2. The controversy over investiture wasn't settled until:

A. the Fourth Lateran Council.
B. the Concordat of Worms.
C. the Battle of Hastings.
D. Henry IV repented.

3. Charlemagne respected the independence of the Church, but Otto:

A. honored the Church more.
B. respected the Church also.
C. merely wanted to control it.
D. was a clergyman.

4. One of the greatest debates of the Middle Ages was:

A. whether or not God exists.
B. how the relationship between the Church and the state ought to look.
C. which horses were the fastest.
D. if women should work for the same wages as men.

5. Otto pressured the Roman Church to allow him the special right of:

A. selecting the pope.
B. saying Mass.
C. having a special audience with the pope.
D. choosing the name of an important cathedral.

True or False?

Directions: In the blank beside each statement, write "T" if the statement is *True* or "F" if the statement is *False*. Each correct answer is worth 5 points. 25 possible points.

_____ 1. Pope Gregory VII excommunicated Emperor Henry IV.

_____ 2. After Henry repented at Canossa, there was peace between the pope and emperor.

_____ 3. Otto the Great was the first Holy Roman emperor.

_____ 4. Some of the popes of the age cared more about politics and power than the care of souls.

_____ 5. After three days at Canossa, Pope Gregory was still not convinced of the emperor's sincerity and would not absolve him of his crimes against the Church.

CHAPTER 15
The Medieval Church

Perfect Score: 100   Your Score: _____

Multiple Choice

Directions: For each numbered item, circle the letter beside the choice (A, B, C, or D) that best answers the question or completes the statement. Circle only one choice per item. Each correct answer is worth 5 points. 25 possible points.

1. The heart of Christian culture in Europe had always been:

A. the Rosary.
B. the monasteries.
C. St. Bernard of Clairvaux.
D. fasting.

2. There were many arguments in the medieval Church over the best way to observe Benedict's rule, which led to:

A. schism.
B. division among Christians.
C. the pope calling for an ecumenical council.
D. the founding of several new religious orders.

3. The greatest preacher of the Middle Ages was:

A. Pope Gelasius.
B. St. Paul.
C. St. Bernard of Clairvaux.
D. St. Augustine of Hippo.

4. This Council defined the transformation of the bread and wine into the Body and Blood of Christ at Mass, taught Catholics should go to confession and receive Communion at least once per year at Easter, condemned certain heresies, and put an end to other abuses.

A. the Fourth Lateran Council
B. the Council of Nicaea
C. the Second Vatican Council
D. the Concordat of Worms

5. St. Bernard of Clairvaux wrote the rule for the:

A. Knights Hospitallers.
B. Cistercians.
C. Templar Knights.
D. Carthusians.

True or False?

Directions: In the blank beside each statement, write "T" if the statement is *True* or "F" if the statement is *False*. Each correct answer is worth 5 points. 75 possible points.

_____ 1. Medieval Christians were not good at practicing their faith.

_____ 2. There were many associations, lay and religious, that were dedicated to taking care of the poor and to good works.

_____ 3. It is said that mothers used to hide their sons when St. Bernard came to town because he preached so eloquently on the joys of the religious life that men who heard him would become monks.

_____ 4. In the High Middle Ages, the Church was not governed by bishops in union with the pope.

_____ 5. The medieval Church did not always have the best leaders.

_____ 6. In the areas where Christianity flourished, the whole culture was transformed into a Christian society.

_____ 7. Christians in the Middle Ages would sometimes go to see plays about religious themes in the town square.

_____ 8. People learned little about the Faith from the art and architecture.

_____ 9. Medieval Catholics cared little about hearing sermons.

_____ 10. St. Bernard was a member of the new Cistercian order.

_____ 11. One of Bernard's most famous miracles happened in the city of Foigny, when he killed all the flies in a church by excommunicating them.

_____ 12. Christianity began as a tiny little sect in Palestine during the height of the Roman Empire and grew impressively.

_____ 13. Medieval civilization was rooted in the Christian faith, which meant it was always perfect.

_____ 14. In the Middle Ages, a bishop could be in charge of more than one diocese.

_____ 15. Those who could read could go to the nearest monastic library and study the Bible or lives of the saints.

CHAPTER 16
Knighthood and Medieval Warfare

Perfect Score: 100   Your Score: _____

Matching

Directions: In each blank beside a phrase, write the letter of the term that is described by that phrase. Each item is worth 5 points. 50 possible points.

A. knight
B. page
C. squire
D. heraldry
E. vassals

F. chivalry
G. St. Louis IX
H. crossbow
I. skirmishers
J. castle

_____ 1. During the seven years a boy would serve in the household of his master, he was called a _____.

_____ 2. the symbols and colors of noble families

_____ 3. the most famous knight-king of the Middle Ages

_____ 4. a man, usually of noble birth, who served his lord in battle as a mounted warrior

_____ 5. large, disorganized groups of men armed with long knives, slings, and clubs

_____ 6. those who served or pledged loyalty to the lord

_____ 7. a very large fortress made of stone that housed a lord and his family, and often many of his knights as well

_____ 8. This is like a bow and arrow attached to a stock and fired like a gun.

_____ 9. This was the last step before becoming a knight.

_____ 10. a code of conduct that guided how knights were to act

True or False?

Directions: In the blank beside each statement, write "T" if the statement is *True* or "F" if the statement is *False*. Each correct answer is worth 5 points. 50 possible points.

_____ 1. In a knighting ceremony, the lord would tap the squire on the shoulders with a sword or sometimes tap him lightly on the cheek.

_____ 2. Knights were trained for war from the age of twenty.

_____ 3. A knight would be expected to serve his master faithfully and be a model of courage and virtue.

_____ 4. If a squire distinguished himself—for example, by saving his lord's life or defeating a host of enemies—the lord could ask him to kneel and make him a knight right there on the battlefield.

_____ 5. Besides knights, a medieval army typically had skirmishers, foot soldiers, and archers.

_____ 6. Using a bow well did not require much training.

_____ 7. The castle hall was often the scene of crowded dinners and merrymaking.

_____ 8. The castle was the center of social life for the nobility.

_____ 9. The evening before the knighting ceremony, the squire would spend the entire night awake praying in the chapel.

_____ 10. A crossbow bolt could not pierce the armor of a knight.

CHAPTER 17
Reconquista

Perfect Score: 100   Your Score: _____

Matching

Directions: In each blank beside a phrase, write the letter of the term that is described by that phrase. Each item is worth 5 points. 50 possible points.

A. Moors
B. Pelayo
C. Asturias
D. Andalusia
E. Reconquista

F. Santiago
G. Santiago de Compostela
H. Castile
I. St. Fernando III
J. Granada

_____ 1. Devotion to St. James was greatest in this kingdom.

_____ 2. the Muslim part of Spain

_____ 3. Muslim warriors who crossed over into Spain from Africa and overran the Christian Visigothic kingdoms in the early 700s

_____ 4. the last Moorish city in Spain, which fell to the Spaniards in the year 1492

_____ 5. the centuries-long struggle of the Spanish Christians to retake their lands from the Moors

_____ 6. led a small band of Christians into hiding in the mountains in northern Spain

_____ 7. the biggest shrine in Spain, dedicated to St. James; a popular destination for Christian pilgrims

_____ 8. the Spanish name for St. James the Apostle

_____ 9. the most renowned king of the Reconquista, who won back more land from the Muslims than any other Christian lord

_____ 10. At first, this was the only Christian kingdom in Muslim Spain.

True or False?

Directions: In the blank beside each statement, write "T" if the statement is *True* or "F" if the statement is *False*. Each correct answer is worth 5 points. 50 possible points.

_____ 1. By the time St. Fernando III died, much of Spain had been reconquered by Christians.

_____ 2. The Christians of Andalusia were allowed to express their faith openly.

_____ 3. The Christians never drove the Moors out of Spain.

_____ 4. The Moors were always divided amongst themselves, which made it hard for them to stand up to the Christians in the long run.

_____ 5. The most popular saint in Spain was St. Peter.

_____ 6. After besieging Coimbra for some time without success, King Fernando of Castile made a pilgrimage to the shrine of Santiago de Compostela to pray for assistance.

_____ 7. The apparition of St. James to the Greek pilgrim at the battle of Coimbra is one of Spain's best-known stories about the love of St. James for the people of Castile.

_____ 8. The Moors preferred to put themselves under the authority of a Moorish prince rather than King Fernando.

_____ 9. According to tradition, St. James brought Christianity to Spain in the Roman times.

_____ 10. Christian missionaries who tried to tell Muslims about Jesus were beheaded. Christians could often be taken away and sold as slaves in North Africa.

CHAPTER 18
Literature of the Middle Ages

Perfect Score: 100   Your Score: _____

Matching

Directions: In each blank beside a phrase, write the letter of the term that is described by that phrase. Each item is worth 5 points. 75 possible points.

A. literature
B. hagiographies
C. annals
D. epics
E. Beowulf
F. chansons de geste
G. Song of Roland
H. romance

I. Sir Gawain and the Green Knight
J. troubadour
K. Divine Comedy
L. Geoffrey Chaucer
M. Florence
N. Arthurian legends
O. Charlemagne

_____ 1. the most famous of the *chansons de geste*, the tales of the brave Frankish warriors

_____ 2. an imaginary account of Dante's pilgrimage through the afterlife

_____ 3. histories of everything that happened in the monastery or kingdom in the year

_____ 4. a story in which a person faced some test of their character or had to overcome some trial to prove their worth

_____ 5. One of the most popular medieval epics, this was a story named after a hero who comes to Denmark to destroy a terrible monster that is troubling the Danish king.

_____ 6. poems about warrior-heroes

_____ 7. stories that told of the lives, virtues, and miracles of a saint

_____ 8. Dante was exiled from this city.

_____ 9. One of the most famous examples of a medieval romance was this story about a mysterious visitor to the court of King Arthur.

_____ 10. all the written works a civilization produces

_____ 11. Some of the earliest medieval French literature was called this French phrase that means "Tales of Deeds."

_____ 12. an Englishman, most famous for his work the *Canterbury Tales*

_____ 13. Some of the most beloved of all medieval romances, these were stories about Arthur and the knights of the Round Table.

_____ 14. In the song of Roland, Roland is a knight in the service of this king.

_____ 15. a kind of wandering poet who would recite his poems for nobility, often accompanied by a lute or some musical instrument

True or False?

Directions: In the blank beside each statement, write "T" if the statement is *True* or "F" if the statement is *False*. Each correct answer is worth 5 points. 25 possible points.

_____ 1. Dante Alighieri wrote poetry about heaven, hell, and purgatory.

_____ 2. Just about everybody in the Middle Ages could read.

_____ 3. At first, medieval stories were recited by poets.

_____ 4. Romances were always about people falling in love.

_____ 5. Dante was a decent poet; none of his poetry ever became truly famous though.

CHAPTER 19
Farms, Villages, and Cities

Perfect Score: 100   Your Score: _____

Matching

Directions: In each blank beside a phrase, write the letter of the term that is described by that phrase. Each item is worth 5 points. 25 possible points.

A. ale   D. farms
B. serfs   E. nobility
C. guild

_____ 1. a group of master craftsmen who set standards of quality and pricing for certain products, as well as decided who was and was not skilled enough to work in a trade

_____ 2. a kind of beer that everybody drank in the Middle Ages, sometimes even young people

_____ 3. Most medieval people worked on these.

_____ 4. Most land in the Middle Ages was owned by these people.

_____ 5. peasants who did not own their farms and cottages and were bound to the land they worked for their lord

True or False?

Directions: In the blank beside each statement, write "T" if the statement is *True* or "F" if the statement is *False*. Each correct answer is worth 5 points. 75 possible points.

_____ 1. Medieval peasants' last names often explained where they lived or what their profession was.

_____ 2. Most medieval farmers filled all of their fields as much as possible with crops every year.

_____ 3. Medieval Europe had an excellent system of roads.

_____ 4. A serf could be released from his duties to his noble lord if he remained in the city for over one year.

_____ 5. Throughout the Middle Ages, cities got less and less important.

_____ 6. Craftsmen who had smellier, messier, or noisier trades—like tanners (who made leather) or papermakers—had their shops outside the city walls.

_____ 7. Guilds made sure pricing was fair and people got quality products for their money.

_____ 8. London and Paris became the largest cities in western Europe.

_____ 9. Ale had a lot of alcohol in it, just like modern beer.

_____ 10. Medieval farms were very long and narrow, like little strips.

_____ 11. Some of each peasant family's crops would go to their lord, while some would go to feed their families.

_____ 12. Cities were never granted special privileges by kings and emperors.

_____ 13. The streets of medieval cities were narrow and zigzagging, sometimes made of stone but more often just mud and dirt.

_____ 14. Fire was rarely a danger in medieval cities.

_____ 15. All sorts of craftsmen could be found inside the city.

CHAPTER 20
Architecture of the Medieval World

Perfect Score: 100   Your Score: _____

True or False?

Directions: In the blank beside each statement, write "T" if the statement is *True* or "F" if the statement is *False*. Each correct answer is worth 5 points. 50 possible points.

_____ 1. Secular buildings were built for religious use.

_____ 2. While important buildings such as churches and castles were built of stone, most medieval buildings were made of wood.

_____ 3. As the Roman emperors began to support the Catholic Church, they often gave secular buildings as gifts to the Church to be used for worship.

_____ 4. Everything in a Gothic church was very rounded.

_____ 5. Advances in construction made it possible to create larger window spaces in Gothic churches.

_____ 6. Gothic churches are known for their stained glass windows.

_____ 7. None of the great Gothic cathedrals are still in existence today.

_____ 8. Churches were always built in the shape of a triangle.

_____ 9. The first basilicas were built in the old Roman style.

_____ 10. Gothic churches were very tall.

Matching

Directions: In each blank beside a phrase, write the letter of the term that is described by that phrase. Each item is worth 5 points. 50 possible points.

A. façade
B. fleches
C. stained glass
D. flying buttresses
E. architecture

F. "Bibles in stone"
G. St. John Lateran
H. basilicas
I. Romanesque
J. Gothic

_____ 1. freestanding pillars outside of a Gothic church connected by arches to give extra support to the walls

_____ 2. the front of a church

_____ 3. originally large secular buildings that the Romans used, which were often turned into large city churches in the Christian era

_____ 4. This church architecture of the later Middle Ages was able to support larger windows because of its ribbed vaults and flying buttresses.

_____ 5. a nickname for churches in the Middle Ages due to all the great stories of the Old and New Testaments depicted in the carvings, statues, and windows of the church

_____ 6. the style of the churches of the early Middle Ages, which had massive, thick walls to hold up their heavy roofs

_____ 7. Pope Sylvester had a magnificent palace—that Constantine gave him— renovated and turned it into this beautiful church.

_____ 8. a type of colored glass that would produce marvelous patterns of color and light inside the church when the sunlight shined through

_____ 9. the way buildings are designed, built, and decorated

_____ 10. pointed spires named after the French word for arrow since they reminded people of gigantic arrows pointing into the sky

CHAPTER 21
The Mendicants

Perfect Score: 100   Your Score: _____

True or False?

Directions: In the blank beside each statement, write "T" if the statement is *True* or "F" if the statement is *False*. Each correct answer is worth 5 points. 50 possible points.

_____ 1. The thirteenth century was a perfect time to live in.

_____ 2. The Franciscans were more or less the same as the Benedictine monks.

_____ 3. Some people initially suspected that Francis was leading people into heresy.

_____ 4. Pope Innocent III was told in a dream from God to approve of the order that Francis had started.

_____ 5. Young Francis lived a carefree life of feasting, drinking, and having parties with his friends.

_____ 6. The first Franciscans lived in monasteries.

_____ 7. Francis was canonized as a saint only two years after his death, one of the quickest canonizations in history.

_____ 8. It did not matter to Dominic if his friars studied theology or not.

_____ 9. Dominic sold his clothes, possessions, and even his manuscripts to feed the hungry.

_____ 10. Francis went to Egypt to try to convert the Muslim sultan.

Matching

Directions: In each blank beside a phrase, write the letter of the term that is described by that phrase. Each item is worth 5 points. 50 possible points.

A. San Damiano
B. Clare
C. friar
D. mendicant order
E. stigmata

F. canon
G. Order of Preachers
H. St. Francis
I. St. Dominic
J. Order of the Friars Minor

_____ 1. One day, as Francis prayed deeply, the crucifix above the altar began to speak to him in this old, ruined chapel near Assisi.

_____ 2. He believed that heretics could only be won back to the Faith by men who showed real holiness, simplicity, and discipline.

_____ 3. a young girl of Assisi who was inspired to found an order of nuns after the example of Francis

_____ 4. comes from a Latin word for begging; means a religious order that survives from begging

_____ 5. the name St. Dominic gave to the order he founded

_____ 6. a kind of monk attached to the service of a bishop

_____ 7. the wounds of Christ miraculously imprinted on the body of a saint such as Francis

_____ 8. a Latin word that means "brother"

_____ 9. He gave up the life of feasting and began preaching a life of simplicity and poverty in the streets.

_____ 10. Francis called his mendicant order this, but everyone referred to them as Franciscans after their founder Francis.

CHAPTER 22
Medieval Universities

Perfect Score: 100   Your Score: _____

Matching

Directions: In each blank beside a phrase, write the letter of the term that is described by that phrase. Each item is worth 5 points. 50 possible points.

A. Trivium   F. charter
B. Quadrivium   G. St. Albert the Great
C. liberal arts   H. Disputatio
D. Latin   I. St. Thomas Aquinas
E. university   J. *Summa Theologiae*

_____ 1. The three courses of the Trivium and the four of the Quadrivium together make up this.

_____ 2. This was studied by older students, and it consisted of arithmetic (math), geometry, music, and astronomy.

_____ 3. a type of medieval school organized for higher learning

_____ 4. was a professor at many universities, as well as a famous theologian and scientist

_____ 5. a kind of argument between professors at a university that happened regularly in the evenings

_____ 6. a document giving the university independence from any bishop or lord

_____ 7. This was studied by younger students; it consisted of the three subjects of grammar (right use of words), logic (right thinking), and rhetoric (right speaking).

_____ 8. a famous book by St. Thomas Aquinas written for students of theology

_____ 9. This saintly Dominican who was a student to St. Albert was supposed to become a Benedictine abbot, but he defied his parents' wishes even after they tried to get him to change his mind by locking him in a tower.

_____ 10. All classes at a university were taught in this language.

True or False?

Directions: In the blank beside each statement, write "T" if the statement is _True_ or "F" if the statement is _False_. Each correct answer is worth 5 points. 50 possible points.

_____ 1. The _Summa Theologiae_ was written in a question and answer format.

_____ 2. Before the invention of printing, books were still cheap and easy to come by.

_____ 3. St. Thomas Aquinas was a professor of theology.

_____ 4. Usually, only the children of nobility or those destined for service in the Church would be taught to read.

_____ 5. The liberal arts were called "liberal" because they belong in a library.

_____ 6. Usually boys and girls both attended monastic schools.

_____ 7. Charlemagne passed a law ordering every bishop to establish a school in his diocese.

_____ 8. At the University of Paris, every student received a clerical habit and was given minor orders.

_____ 9. The cathedral schools were run by the clergy.

_____ 10. Cathedral schools received a charter from the pope.

CHAPTER 23
The Heretical Movements

Perfect Score: 100   Your Score: _____

Matching

Directions: In each blank beside a phrase, write the letter of the term that is described by that phrase. Each item is worth 5 points. 50 possible points.

A. heresy
B. Berengar
C. transubstantiation
D. Petrobrusians
E. Peter of Bruis

F. Arnold of Brescia
G. Cathars/Albigensians
H. St. Dominic
I. the Rosary
J. the Inquisition

_____ 1. the change of the bread and wine into Jesus's Body and Blood

_____ 2. a French monk who taught that Jesus Christ was not truly present in the Blessed Sacrament

_____ 3. came to southern France to preach to the Cathars in hopes of winning them back to the true Faith of Christ

_____ 4. the most well-known heretics of the Middle Ages who believed flesh was evil and the human body was created by an evil spirit and only the soul was from God

_____ 5. an Italian monk who taught that the Church should not own any property and that it was wrong for the Church to govern the Papal States

_____ 6. a legal process aimed at identifying heretics and encouraging them to repent

_____ 7. He taught that Christians should not build churches and that one should not pray for the souls in purgatory, but his most notable teaching was that crosses and crucifixes should be destroyed.

_____ 8. the followers of Peter of Bruis

_____ 9. a Greek word that means "wrong thinking" and is used to refer to teachings other than those accepted by the Church

_____ 10. St. Dominic traveled throughout the lands of Cathars preaching and teaching them to pray this.

Multiple Choice

Directions: For each numbered item, circle the letter beside the choice (A, B, C, or D). that best answers the question or completes the statement. Circle only one choice per item. Each correct answer is worth 5 points. 25 possible points.

1. Heretics who were discovered during the Inquisition would be given a chance to repent and do penance. If they did not, the Church would:

A. turn them over to the secular authorities.
B. torture them cruelly.
C. banish them from the land.
D. make them do penance.

2. While the Church taught that the Eucharist is the Body and Blood of Jesus, Berengar taught that it was:

A. just special holy bread.
B. from the Devil and thus sinful to consume.
C. only a symbol of Jesus.
D. the Body and Blood of Jesus.

3. Wherever the Petrobrusians went, they

A. tore down crosses and crucifixes and burned them in gigantic bonfires.
B. taught the gospel.
C. were welcomed.
D. slaughtered innocent people.

4. When their most deeply held beliefs were mocked and ridiculed by heretics, medieval people could react with:

A. patience.
B. intellectual arguments.
C. tolerance.
D. violence.

5. Cathars tended to reject marriage because:

A. they thought that adultery wasn't wrong.
B. marriage led to children and the Cathars did not want to bring more imprisoned spirits into the world.
C. they held a tradition that marriage was an institute founded by an evil demon.
D. marriage produced children and mothers who were dependent on society to take care of them.

True or False?

Directions: In the blank beside each statement, write "T" if the statement is *True* or "F" if the statement is *False*. Each correct answer is worth 5 points. 25 possible points.

_____ 1. Medieval heresy was just a religious problem; the government never really got mixed up in it at all.

_____ 2. One of the officials of Pope Innocent III was murdered by Cathars in France.

_____ 3. Berengar's teachings were condemned by several Church synods.

_____ 4. Berengar never realized he was wrong about transubstantiation and never repented.

_____ 5. Wherever Christianity spread, there were always heresies challenging its teachings.

CHAPTER 24
Church and State Collide

Perfect Score: 100   Your Score: _____

Multiple Choice

Directions: For each numbered item, circle the letter beside the choice (A, B, C, or D) that best answers the question or completes the statement. Circle only one choice per item. Each correct answer is worth 5 points. 25 possible points.

1. The Investiture Controversy was an argument over:

A. how much money the Templar Knights ought to have.
B. how much control lay people should have over the Church.
C. whether or not it is morally permissible for bankers to charge interest.
D. whether or not the Eucharist really is Jesus's Body and Blood.

2. Pope Adrian did not like having to ask Frederick for help, but he had no choice. Frederick agreed to help the pope win back Rome. In return, the pope:

A. gave him a plenary indulgence.
B. let him ordain bishops.
C. crowned him Holy Roman emperor.
D. provided supplies.

3. The new pope, Alexander III, pressured Emperor Frederick to give up his wars. In response, Frederick:

A. tried to attack Alexander by supporting an antipope.
B. put more effort into war.
C. tried to assassinate the pope.
D. rejected the Church.

4. The popes did not get along well with Frederick Barbarossa. They got on even worse with his grandson:

A. Henry V.
B. Frederick II.
C. Philip IV.
D. Alexander.

5. Pope Alexander III excommunicated Emperor Frederick for:

A. unjustly killing five thousand innocent people.
B. meddling with Church affairs.
C. making alliances with Muslims.
D. his support of the antipope.

True or False?

Directions: In the blank beside each statement, write "T" if the statement is *True* or "F" if the statement is *False*. Each correct answer is worth 5 points. 75 possible points.

_____ 1. While crossing a river in Asia Minor, Emperor Frederick Barbarossa fell from his horse and drowned.

_____ 2. The Third Crusade was not able to recapture Jerusalem.

_____ 3. There is a German legend that Frederick Barbarossa is not dead but sleeping under a mountain in Germany.

_____ 4. Frederick II was excommunicated for breaking his promise to the pope to go on crusade.

_____ 5. Frederick II did everything he could to try to hurt the pope.

_____ 6. The Church called Frederick II the Antichrist and a persecutor of the Christians.

_____ 7. Philip IV wanted to tax the French church to pay for the war with England.

_____ 8. Pope Boniface wrote a letter telling King Philip he was absolutely not allowed to tax the Church without the Church's permission.

_____ 9. King Philip believed that he owed obedience to the papacy.

_____ 10. Philip decided to go after the Templar Knights for their money.

_____ 11. King Philip issued a secret order to his soldiers to arrest all the Templars on a single day.

_____ 12. Templar Grandmaster Jacques de Molay was able to escape King Philip's persecution by fleeing to England.

_____ 13. Frederick Barbarossa wanted to regain imperial control of the Church.

_____ 14. An *antipope* is a man who claims to be pope but is not the real pope.

_____ 15. Frederick Barbarossa was never an opponent of the Church.

CHAPTER 25
Avignon and the Great Western Schism

Perfect Score: 100   Your Score: _____

Matching

Directions: In each blank beside a phrase, write the letter of the term that is described by that phrase. Each item is worth 5 points. 50 possible points.

A. Avignon   F. deposed
B. St. Vincent Ferrer   G. Council of Pisa
C. St. Elizabeth of Portugal   H. Council of Constance
D. Third Order   I. Great Western Schism
E. St. Bridget of Sweden   J. St. Catherine of Siena

_____ 1. the period in Church history when there were multiple men claiming to be pope

_____ 2. a kind of branch that the Dominicans, Franciscans, and other religious orders established for laypeople

_____ 3. a place in southern France where the popes lived for much of the fourteenth century

_____ 4. a queen known for her modesty, humility, and generosity

_____ 5. She was married at a young age to a very pious husband; after his death, she founded a religious order. She also urged the pope to return to Rome, but to no avail.

_____ 6. She was a holy Third Order Dominican who was a mystic and Doctor of the Church. She encouraged Pope Gregory XI to return to Rome and received the stigmata.

_____ 7. a Spanish Dominican preacher who committed the entire Bible to memory and traveled throughout Europe preaching and performing thousands of miracles

_____ 8. At this council, two of the popes agreed to quit; the third pope who refused to quit was excommunicated, and a new successor of Peter, Pope Martin V, was chosen.

_____ 9. declared both the Roman and Avignon popes deposed and elected a new pope, but still did not solve the schism

_____ 10. to be removed from one's position

True or False?

Directions: In the blank beside each statement, write "T" if the statement is _True_ or "F" if the statement is _False_. Each correct answer is worth 5 points. 50 possible points.

_____ 1. The cardinals said the election of Pope Urban was valid.

_____ 2. At one point, there were three men who each claimed to be pope.

_____ 3. All the saints in the Middle Ages were priests and monks.

_____ 4. Most historians and theologians teach that the popes at Rome were always the real popes.

_____ 5. The people of Rome were suspicious of Clement because he was French.

_____ 6. Many Catholics strongly disapproved of the papal court moving to Avignon.

_____ 7. The French kings tried to make the Avignon popes their puppets.

_____ 8. Most Christians were not concerned about the Church's political affairs.

_____ 9. God never abandons His Church.

_____ 10. The Church is both divine and human.

CHAPTER 26
Medieval Law

Perfect Score: 100   Your Score: _____

Matching

Directions: In each blank beside a phrase, write the letter of the term that is described by that phrase. Each item is worth 5 points. 75 possible points.

A. natural law
B. laws
C. royal law
D. canon law
E. *Decretals*
F. guild
G. apprentice
H. journeyman

I. masterpiece
J. manorial courts
K. bribe
L. justice
M. bailiff
N. pillory
O. God's eternal law

_____ 1. the laws and traditions that are used to govern the Church

_____ 2. when everybody receives what is rightfully theirs

_____ 3. the order and design of God found in nature

_____ 4. A journeyman would become a master by producing one of these, a superb work that he had to show the guild to prove he had mastered his craft.

_____ 5. the law of the kings

_____ 6. rules that the governing authorities put in place to regulate people's actions and protect the common good

_____ 7. a kind of wooden structure with holes through which someone being punished for a crime would have to stick his head and hands

_____ 8. A monk named Gratian sorted through all the many centuries of canon law and put it together into these three books.

_____ 9. someone training to enter a guild; they usually did not get paid except in food, shelter, and the skill he learned from the master

_____ 10. gatherings at the hall of the local lord where the lord would judge cases

_____ 11. a group of master craftsmen who set standards of quality and pricing for certain products

_____ 12. medieval people believed that this was the greatest law

_____ 13. an officer who administered the laws of the lord and helped the lord in his decisions

_____ 14. a craftsman who would still work under a master, but was skilled enough to get paid for his work.

_____ 15. to give certain judgments in exchange for money

True or False?

Directions: In the blank beside each statement, write "T" if the statement is *True* or "F" if the statement is *False*. Each correct answer is worth 5 points. 25 possible points.

_____ 1. When medieval people made laws, they wanted their laws to reflect God's laws.

_____ 2. By the High Middle Ages, Christianity was over a thousand years old.

_____ 3. A town or village usually had its own council that was able to establish rules of conduct.

_____ 4. If a master began turning out sloppy work, or did not treat his customers well, or charged too much or too little for his work, the guild could do nothing about it.

_____ 5. The guild was able to make its own laws and enforce them on its members.

CHAPTER 27
The Black Death Strikes

Perfect Score: 100   Your Score: _____

Matching

Directions: In each blank beside a phrase, write the letter of the term that is described by that phrase. Each item is worth 5 points. 50 possible points.

A. Black Death   F. Bubonic Plague
B. plagues   G. Paracelsus
C. bacteria   H. rats
D. humours   I. quarantine
E. Galen   J. Danse Macabre

_____ 1. another name for the Black Death

_____ 2. animals that brought the plague to Europe

_____ 3. another name for the four basic fluids people thought the body was composed of

_____ 4. a disease that spread throughout Europe in the middle of the 1300s and killed millions of people

_____ 5. tiny organisms that can cause sickness; medieval people did not know about them

_____ 6. diseases that spread rapidly and kill many people

_____ 7. a late medieval German doctor who believed that sickness came from poisoned dust that came to earth from the stars

_____ 8. This means "Dance of Death" and was a common theme in late medieval art, usually showing skeletons dancing. The purpose of this was to remind people that, whether they were poor or wealthy, death came to everybody equally.

_____ 9. to be sealed in one's house and forbidden from coming out until one is no longer sick

_____ 10. Most medieval doctors followed the theories of this old Roman doctor.

True or False?

Directions: In the blank beside each statement, write "T" if the statement is *True* or "F" if the statement is *False*. Each correct answer is worth 5 points. 50 possible points.

_____ 1. The plague caused people to have greater concern for the salvation of their souls.

_____ 2. A person or family with the plague might be quarantined.

_____ 3. Death was a rare theme in drawings and paintings during the time of the Black Death.

_____ 4. Medieval people knew little about how disease spread.

_____ 5. Black lumps around the armpits, neck, or thighs were a main symptom of the Black Death.

_____ 6. Very often, people who had the plague died within a week.

_____ 7. The medievals knew all about germs and the scientific reasons why sicknesses happened.

_____ 8. With so many peasants dead, there were fewer workers available to work for the nobles.

_____ 9. The Black Death was brought into Europe by merchant ships that were carrying rats.

_____ 10. In France and England, peasants revolted and demanded better wages and fairer rents, causing many of the old feudal customs to begin to vanish.

CHAPTER 28
The Hundred Years War

Perfect Score: 100 Your Score: _____

Matching

Directions: In each blank beside a phrase, write the letter of the term that is described by that phrase. Each item is worth 5 points. 25 possible points.

A. King Philip IV

B. martyr

C. longbows

D. St. Joan of Arc

E. Rheims

_____ 1. When the English and the French armies fought, the English would use these to shower arrows down upon the French knights.

_____ 2. The French prince Charles was crowned king of France here.

_____ 3. the powerful but wicked king of France who had three sons, each of whom ruled for a little while after him

_____ 4. This young girl was called by God to lead the French into battle in the name of Jesus.

_____ 5. The Church studied the trial of Joan of Arc and declared that Joan was innocent of all charges made against her and that she was a _____.

True or False?

Directions: In the blank beside each statement, write "T" if the statement is *True* or "F" if the statement is *False*. Each correct answer is worth 5 points. 75 possible points.

_____ 1. St. Joan received visions on multiple occasions throughout her childhood.

_____ 2. The arrival of St. Joan made little difference for the French in the war against England.

_____ 3. St. Joan of Arc received help from God to fight for France.

_____ 4. The standard of St. Joan featured the names of Jesus and Mary stitched upon it.

_____ 5. The Black Death stopped the war between France and England.

_____ 6. St. Joan was captured by the English and put to death on a charge of heresy and witchcraft.

_____ 7. The English armies were much smaller than the French.

_____ 8. At one point, it seemed that England had won the war.

_____ 9. St. Joan's trial for witchcraft is a good example of a fair trial.

_____ 10. When the English and the French armies fought, the French liked to cluster as many knights together as they could.

_____ 11. Edward III of England claimed that he should inherit the French throne.

_____ 12. After the death of St. Joan, the French no longer had any victories over England.

_____ 13. The French accepted that King Edward of England was the rightful heir to the French throne.

_____ 14. St. Joan of Arc was given a suit of armor to wear into battle.

_____ 15. St. Joan of Arc died at the young age of nineteen.

CHAPTER 29
The Wars of the Roses

Perfect Score: 100   Your Score: _____

Matching

Directions: In each blank beside a phrase, write the letter of the term that is described by that phrase. Each item is worth 5 points. 50 possible points.

A. King Henry VI
B. House of Lancaster
C. House of York
D. Wars of the Roses
E. Richard III

F. Lord Stanley
G. Henry Tudor
H. Bosworth Field
I. King Henry VII
J. the white and red rose

_____ 1. The House of Lancaster united behind this Welsh nobleman who brought an army up the coast of England and marched to attack King Richard III.

_____ 2. Their symbol was a white rose.

_____ 3. This king of England was mentally ill, and many people argued that he should not be king.

_____ 4. the family of Henry VI, whose symbol was a red rose

_____ 5. The war between the Houses of Lancaster and York is called the _____.

_____ 6. When King Richard III threatened to kill this man's son if he did not fight for him, the man responded, "Sire, I have other sons."

_____ 7. the symbol of the House of Tudor, in which the bloodlines of York and Lancaster were joined

_____ 8. He seized the throne after locking his two nephews away in a tower.

_____ 9. Henry Tudor would become known as this when he became king.

_____ 10. The armies of Henry Tudor and King Richard III fought in 1485 at this place.

True or False?

Directions: In the blank beside each statement, write "T" if the statement is *True* or "F" if the statement is *False*. Each correct answer is worth 5 points. 50 possible points.

_____ 1. The princes of the House of York were never seen again.

_____ 2. By the time the Hundred Years' War ended in 1453, England had lost most of its territory in France.

_____ 3. Richard III protected his nephews and raised them up to be good rulers.

_____ 4. King Richard III placed a lot of trust in his nobles.

_____ 5. Instead of protecting the two princes, Richard III had them locked up in a tower.

_____ 6. There was a rebellion against King Richard III.

_____ 7. Richard III thought that many of his nobles liked him.

_____ 8. The death of Richard III at the Battle of Bosworth Field marked the end of the Wars of the Roses.

_____ 9. King Henry VII joined the white rose of York and the red rose of Lancaster together.

____ 10. Richard III wanted the throne for himself.

CHAPTER 30
Medieval Inventions

Perfect Score: 100   Your Score: _____

Matching

Directions: In each blank beside a phrase, write the letter of the term that is described by that phrase. Each item is worth 5 points. 100 possible points.

A. invention
B. Johannes Gutenberg
C. animals
D. Eilmer of Malmesbury
E. Christian faith
F. expensive
G. breast collar
H. waterwheel
I. St. Benedict
J. movable type

K. monks
L. religious
M. mills
N. church steeples and abbey towers
O. Divine Office
P. cities
Q. beer
R. mechanical clock
S. rivers
T. Romans

_____ 1. Before the invention of the printing press, making books was very _____.

_____ 2. The medieval way of harnessing horses was superior to the way these people did it.

_____ 3. Many medieval inventions were created by them.

_____ 4. He invented a hang glider but it crashed when he tested it.

_____ 5. inventor of movable type

_____ 6. These all competed to see who could build the most magnificent clocks.

_____ 7. This encouraged people to be curious about the world.

_____ 8. a division of Psalms prayed by monks

_____ 9. a device or process people create to make their life or work easier

_____ 10. This was originally invented to help monks keep track of their prayers.

_____ 11. The hardest work in the Middle Ages was done by these.

_____ 12. a padded harness worn across a horse's chest

_____ 13. The first mechanical clocks were built in these.

_____ 14. an invention that produced energy from flowing water

_____ 15. Monks invented it when they added hops to malted barley.

_____ 16. The arrangement of the Divine Office went back to him.

_____ 17. where heads of grain were crushed to make flour

_____ 18. The first printed books were all _____.

_____ 19. Waterwheels were built next to these.

_____ 20. It was this invention that made printing easy and inexpensive.

CHAPTER 31
Traders and Explorers

Perfect Score: 100   Your Score: _____

Multiple Choice

Directions: For each numbered item, circle the letter beside the choice (A, B, C, or D) that best answers the question or completes the statement. Circle only one choice per item. Each correct answer is worth 10 points. 100 possible points.

1. This Venetian made a famous journey to the court of Kublai Khan.

A. Gil Eanes
B. Henry the Navigator
C. Marco Polo
D. Bartolomeu Dias

2. These were very rare in medieval Europe; therefore, people paid a lot for them.

A. vegetables
B. spices
C. woolen garments
D. swords

3. Medieval traders were always looking for the best way to get to:

A. Africa.
B. the Muslim kingdoms.
C. Russia.
D. China, Japan, and the Far East.

4. As long as this group was in charge of Asia, Christians could travel safely by land from Europe to China.

A. Mongols
B. Chinese
C. Muslims
D. Venetians

5. The first sea routes around Africa were discovered by sailors from:

A. Spain.
B. England.
C. Portugal.
D. Venice.

6. The prince who set up a school for navigation was:

A. Marco Polo.
B. King John II.
C. Vasco de Gama.
D. Henry.

7. The famous Portuguese school for navigation was located at:

A. Sagres.
B. Venice.
C. the Cape of Good Hope.
D. Byzantium.

8. For sailing so far around Africa, Prince Henry made this man a knight.

A. Vasco de Gama
B. Marco Polo
C. Gil Eanes
D. Bartolomeu Dias

9. Bartolomeu Dias was the first European explorer to:

A. visit the court of Kublai Khan:
B. make it to China.
C. bring back African plants and animals.
D. round the tip of Africa.

10. In 1498, he rounded the Cape of Good Hope and made it on to India.

A. Vasco de Gama
B. Bartolomeu Dias
C. Gil Eanes
D. Prince Henry the Navigator

CHAPTER 32
The Fall of Constantinople

Perfect Score: 100   Your Score: _____

Matching

Directions: In each blank beside a phrase, write the letter of the term that is described by that phrase. Each item is worth 10 points. 100 possible points.

A. crusaders
B. Byzantium
C. Ottomans
D. Gregory X
E. sultans

F. Mehmed II
G. Constantine XI Paleologos
H. Hagia Sophia
I. Istanbul
J. Lyons and Florence

_____ 1. Constantinople was the capital of this empire.

_____ 2. the name that the Turks gave Constantinople

_____ 3. the last emperor of Constantinople

_____ 4. the pope who invited the Greeks to the Council of Lyon

_____ 5. kings of the Ottoman Turks

_____ 6. The Muslims who conquered Constantinople were _____.

_____ 7. ruler of the Ottoman Turks

_____ 8. two councils where the Catholics and Greeks tried to reunite

_____ 9. the grand church of Constantinople; later turned into a mosque

_____ 10. These Christians once attacked and ruled Constantinople.

CHAPTER 33
The Earliest Days of the Renaissance

Perfect Score: 100   Your Score: _____

Multiple Choice

Directions: For each numbered item, circle the letter beside the choice (A, B, C, or D) that best answers the question or completes the statement. Circle only one choice per item. Each correct answer is worth 5 points. 50 possible points.

1. Ghiberti and Brunelleschi were competing in a contest to:

A. design the dome of St. Peter's Basilica.
B. paint the ceiling of the Sistine Chapel.
C. decorate the doors of the Florence baptistery.
D. paint the Mona Lisa.

2. *Renaissance* means:

A. "reform."
B. "rebirth."
C. "recycle."
D. "retire."

3. During the Renaissance, scholars, monks, theologians, and officials came to western Europe from:

A. France.
B. the Holy Land.
C. China.
D. Greece.

4. During the Renaissance, Christians' knowledge of the Bible was enriched by being able to study it in:

A. Latin.
B. Greek and Hebrew.
C. Greek and Latin.
D. Hebrew and Latin.

5. An image that looks three dimensional, giving the appearance of depth or distance, is said to have:

A. perspective.
B. luminosity.
C. shading.
D. intensity.

6. Mona Lisa, one of the most famous paintings in the world, was painted by:

A. Filippo Brunelleschi.
B. Michelangelo.
C. Leonardo da Vinci.
D. Raphael.

7. This artist spent years decorating the Vatican with frescoes that still astonish visitors today.

A. Michelangelo
B. Leonardi da Vinci
C. Ghiberti
D. Raphael

8. Renaissance engineers rediscovered the technique of making:

A. domes.
B. vaulted arches.
C. buttresses.
D. columns.

9. One of the greatest domes in Christendom, built during the Renaissance, was the dome of:

A. Hagia Sophia in Constantinople.
B. St. Peter's Basilica in Rome.
C. The Florence cathedral.
D. the palace of Venice.

10. Which of the following was *not* something attacked by the heretics of the Renaissance?

A. veneration of relics
B. the culture of Greece and Rome
C. pilgrimages
D. the use of indulgences

True or False?

Directions: In the blank beside each statement, write "T" if the statement is *True* or "F" if the statement is *False*. Each correct answer is worth 5 points. 50 possible points.

_____ 1. The people of the Renaissance were inspired by the cultures of ancient Greece and Rome.

_____ 2. Some of the greatest painters in history lived during the Renaissance.

_____ 3. Medieval art was much more realistic looking than Renaissance art.

_____ 4. The famous baptistery door contest of the year 1400 was held in the city of Florence.

_____ 5. The job of decorating the baptistery doors was eventually given to Brunelleschi.

_____ 6. The Church encouraged the art of the Renaissance.

_____ 7. Michelangelo's most famous works are the biblical paintings on the ceiling of the Sistine Chapel.

_____ 8. During the Renaissance, people read less and were less educated.

_____ 9. The printing press made it easier for heretics to spread their ideas.

_____ 10. Some Renaissance scholars looked down on the Middle Ages and called them the "Dark Ages."

ANSWER KEY

CHAPTER 1—The Christian Empire
Test Book pages 1–4

Multiple Choice
1. A   2. B   3. C   4. B   5. D

True or False?
1. T   2. F   3. F   4. T   5. T

Matching
1. D   2. H   3. A   4. C   5. E   6. J   7. G   8. B   9. I   10. F

CHAPTER 2—The End of the Roman World
Test Book pages 5–6

Matching
1. F   2. H   3. A   4. B   5. E   6. J   7. D   8. G   9. I   10. C

True or False?
1. F   2. F   3. T   4. T   5. F   6. T   7. T   8. T   9. T   10. T

CHAPTER 3—The Age of Justinian
Test Book pages 7–9

Multiple Choice
1. B   2. A   3. C   4. A   5. D   6. A   7. B   8. C   9. B   10. A   11. D   12. B
13. C   14. B   15. A

True or False?
1. T   2. F   3. T   4. T   5. F

CHAPTER 4—The Rule of St. Benedict
Test Book pages 11–12

Matching

1. G   2. C   3. I   4. J   5. A   6. F   7. E   8. H   9. B   10. D

True or False?

1. F   2. T   3. T   4. F   5. T   6. F   7. T   8. F   9. F   10. T

CHAPTER 5—The Irish Missions
Test Book pages 13–14

Matching

1. A   2. G   3. B   4. D   5. J   6. F   7. C   8. H   9. I   10. E

True or False?

1. T   2. T   3. T   4. F   5. T   6. F   7. T   8. T   9. F   10. T

CHAPTER 6—The Church's Eldest Daughter
Test Book pages 15–17

Matching

1. G   2. C   3. I   4. E   5. A   6. F   7. D   8. H   9. J   10. B

Multiple Choice

1. A   2. D   3. B   4. A   5. C

True or False?

1. T   2. F   3. F   4. T   5. T

CHAPTER 7—The Coming of the Moors
Test Book pages 19–20

True or False?

1. T   2. T   3. F   4. T   5. F

Matching

1. D   2. C   3. A   4. N   5. F   6. H   7. G   8. I   9. B   10. J   11. K   12. E
13. L   14. O   15. M

CHAPTER 8—The Carolingians
Test Book pages 21–23

True or False?
1. T   2. F   3. T   4. T   5. F   6. T   7. T   8. F   9. F   10. T

Multiple Choice
1. B   2. D   3. C   4. B   5. A   6. A   7. D   8. A   9. C   10. B

CHAPTER 9—The Conversion of Europe
Test Book pages 25–26

Matching
1. D   2. H   3. C   4. A   5. E   6. J   7. G   8. F   9. I   10. B

True or False?
1. F   2. T   3. T   4. T   5. T   6. F   7. T   8. T   9. F   10. T

CHAPTER 10—Anglo-Saxon England
Test Book pages 27–29

Matching
1. E   2. J   3. B   4. D   5. C   6. H   7. G   8. A   9. I   10. F

Multiple Choice
1. A   2. C   3. B   4. A   5. D

True or False?
1. F   2. T   3. F   4. T   5. T

CHAPTER 11—The Normans
Test Book pages 31–32

Matching
1. H   2. B   3. D   4. J   5. E   6. F   7. G   8. C   9. I   10. A

True or False?
1. T   2. F   3. T   4. T   5. F   6. T   7. F   8. T   9. T   10. T

CHAPTER 12—The Norman Conquest of England
Test Book pages 33–36

Matching
1. E   2. B   3. A   4. H   5. C   6. F   7. J   8. G   9. D   10. I

Multiple Choice
1. A   2. C   3. B   4. C   5. C

True or False?
1. F   2. T   3. T   4. F   5. T

CHAPTER 13—The Crusades
Test Book pages 37–39

Matching
1. D   2. F   3. K   4. J   5. I   6. B   7. A   8. H   9. E   10. G   11. O   12. L
13. C   14. N   15. M

Multiple Choice
1. A   2. D   3. A   4. C   5. B

CHAPTER 14—The Investiture Controversy
Test Book pages 41–43

Matching
1. A   2. C   3. J   4. D   5. B   6. F   7. E   8. H   9. I   10. G

Multiple Choice
1. D   2. B   3. C   4. B   5. A

True or False?
1. T   2. F   3. T   4. T   5. F

CHAPTER 15—The Medieval Church
Test Book pages 45–47

Multiple Choice
1. B   2. D   3. C   4. A   5. C

True or False?
1. F   2. T   3. T   4. F   5. T   6. T   7. T   8. F   9. F   10. T   11. T   12. T
13. F   14. T   15. T

CHAPTER 16—Knighthood and Medieval Warfare
Test Book pages 49–50

Matching
1. B   2. D   3. G   4. A   5. I   6. E   7. J   8. H   9. C   10. F

True or False?
1. T   2. F   3. T   4. T   5. T   6. F   7. T   8. T   9. T   10. F

CHAPTER 17—Reconquista
Test Book pages 51–52

Matching
1. H   2. D   3. A   4. J   5. E   6. B   7. G   8. F   9. I   10. C

True or False?
1. T   2. F   3. F   4. T   5. F   6. T   7. T   8. F   9. T   10. T

CHAPTER 18—Literature of the Middle Ages
Test Book pages 53–54

Matching
1. G   2. K   3. C   4. H   5. E   6. D   7. B   8. M   9. I   10. A   11. F   12. L
13. N   14. O   15. J

True or False?
1. T   2. F   3. T   4. F   5. F

CHAPTER 19—Farms, Villages, and Cities
Test Book pages 55–56

Matching
1. C   2. A   3. D   4. E   5. B

True or False?
1. T   2. F   3. F   4. T   5. F   6. T   7. T   8. T   9. F   10. T   11. T   12. F
13. T   14. F   15. T

CHAPTER 20—Architecture of the Medieval World
Test Book pages 57–58

True or False?
1. F   2. T   3. T   4. F   5. T   6. T   7. F   8. F   9. T   10. T

Matching
1. D   2. A   3. H   4. J   5. F   6. I   7. G   8. C   9. E   10. B

CHAPTER 21—The Mendicants
Test Book pages 59–60

True or False?
1. F   2. F   3. T   4. T   5. T   6. F   7. T   8. F   9. T   10. T

Matching
1. A   2. I   3. B   4. D   5. G   6. F   7. E   8. C   9. H   10. J

CHAPTER 22—Medieval Universities
Test Book pages 61–62

Matching
1. C   2. B   3. E   4. G   5. H   6. F   7. A   8. J   9. I   10. D

True or False?
1. T   2. F   3. T   4. T   5. F   6. F   7. T   8. T   9. T   10. F

CHAPTER 23—The Heretical Movements
Test Book pages 63–65

Matching
1. C   2. B   3. H   4. G   5. F   6. J   7. E   8. D   9. A   10. I

Multiple Choice
1. A   2. C   3. A   4. D   5. B

True or False?
1. F   2. T   3. T   4. F   5. T

CHAPTER 24—Church and State Collide
Test Book pages 66–69

Multiple Choice
1. B   2. C   3. A   4. B   5. D

True or False?
1. T   2. F   3. T   4. T   5. T   6. T   7. T   8. T   9. F   10. T   11. T   12. F
13. T   14. T   15. F

CHAPTER 25—Avignon and the Great Western Schism
Test Book pages 71–72

Matching
1. I   2. D   3. A   4. C   5. E   6. J   7. B   8. H   9. G   10. F

True or False?
1. F   2. T   3. F   4. T   5. T   6. T   7. T   8. F   9. T   10. T

CHAPTER 26—Medieval Law
Test Book pages 73–74

Matching
1. D   2. L   3. A   4. I   5. C   6. B   7. N   8. E   9. G   10. J   11. F   12. O
13. M   14. H   15. K

True or False?
1. T   2. T   3. T   4. F   5. T

CHAPTER 27—The Black Death Strikes
Test Book pages 75–76

Matching
1. F   2. H   3. D   4. A   5. C   6. B   7. G   8. J   9. I   10. E

True or False?
1. T   2. T   3. F   4. F   5. T   6. T   7. F   8. T   9. T   10. T

CHAPTER 28—The Hundred Years War
Test Book pages 77–78

Matching
1. C   2. E   3. A   4. D   5. B

True or False?
1. T   2. F   3. T   4. T   5. F   6. T   7. T   8. T   9. F   10. T   11. T   12. F
13. F   14. T   15. T

CHAPTER 29—The Wars of the Roses
Test Book pages 79–80

Matching
1. G   2. C   3. A   4. B   5. D   6. F   7. J   8. E   9. I   10. H

True or False?
1. T   2. T   3. F   4. F   5. T   6. T   7. F   8. T   9. T   10. T

CHAPTER 30—Medieval Inventions
Test Book pages 81–82

Matching
1. F   2. T   3. K   4. D   5. B   6. P   7. E   8. O   9. A   10. R   11. C   12. G
13. N   14. H   15. Q   16. I   17. M   18. L   19. S   20. J

CHAPTER 31—Traders and Explorers
Test Book pages 83–84

Multiple Choice
1. C   2. B   3. D   4. A   5. C   6. D   7. A   8. C   9. D   10. A

CHAPTER 32—The Fall of Constantinople
Test Book page 85

Matching
1. B   2. I   3. G   4. D   5. E   6. C   7. F   8. J   9. H   10. A

CHAPTER 33—The Earliest Days of the Renaissance
Test Book pages 87–89

Multiple Choice
1. C   2. B   3. D   4. B   5. A   6. C   7. D   8. A   9. B   10. B

True or False?
1. T   2. T   3. F   4. T   5. F   6. T   7. T   8. F   9. T   10. T

NOTES

NOTES

NOTES

NOTES

TAN · BOOKS

TAN Books is the Publisher You Can Trust With Your Faith.

TAN Books was founded in 1967 to preserve the spiritual, intellectual, and liturgical traditions of the Catholic Church. At a critical moment in history TAN kept alive the great classics of the Faith and drew many to the Church. In 2008 TAN was acquired by Saint Benedict Press. Today TAN continues to teach and defend the Faith to a new generation of readers.

TAN publishes more than 600 booklets, Bibles, and books. Popular subject areas include theology and doctrine, prayer and the supernatural, history, biography, and the lives of the saints. TAN's line of educational and homeschooling resources is featured at TANHomeschool.com.

TAN publishes under several imprints, including TAN, Neumann Press, ACS Books, and the Confraternity of the Precious Blood. Sister imprints include Saint Benedict Press, Catholic Courses, and Catholic Scripture Study.

For more information about TAN,
or to request a free catalog, visit
TANBooks.com

Or call us toll-free at
(800) 437-5876